To my inspiration for this book:

my children

Emily, Tina and Charlie.

This has been written in the hope that others can find support and comfort amongst the chaos that alcohol can bring to lives.

I love my Mum and Dad.

My name is Katie. I'm 13 years old now, an only child with parents who love me very much. I live in a detached house where I have a big bedroom and music room of my own. I should be really happy living here.

My Dad is a dentist and my Mum is a teacher at my High School. Having both parents working means we can have really good holidays twice a year – my friends at school tell me how lucky I am. I ought to be more grateful for my middle class life.

Sometimes Mum and Dad have friends round for drinks. When I see "PARTY" written on the kitchen calendar I usually get a nervous tummy days before it's about to happen. I've been like that for as long as I can remember.

I like seeing Mum and Dad's friends;
but I don't like it when they all go home at the end of the night.

The night usually starts well – my nervous tummy is there but not causing me to run to the toilet too often! Mum is a great hostess, everyone says so. She always makes sure everyone has a full glass of whatever they're drinking. I've not met anyone who doesn't love my Mum.

All my friends at school tell me what a great teacher she is too, and how lucky I am to have her as my Mum. I do love her. They would never believe me if I told them about the parties and what happens when she's been drinking. I just pretend my life is great and everything is just the way everyone in the outside world thinks it is. There doesn't seem much point in disappointing them or spoiling their image of my life and my Mum's drinking.

I try to hide my worries about Mum, but I think my Dad notices: at the parties he always looks a bit nervous too. On more than one occasion I've seen her pouring herself a glass in the kitchen, drinking it down very quickly then topping it up again before joining the others. She always seems to need to drink more than anyone else. When I see her doing that I usually start to feel nervous. I've seen this pattern so many times before and I know it won't end well.

I get very tired at school after one of Mum and Dad's parties.

My tummy aches and I need to get out of the stuffy classroom. I find it really hard listening to the others talk about their weekends – I usually make something up about going swimming or having a quiet time. The truth is that I was scared watching Mum change with each mouthful of wine she had on Saturday night; wondering when she would get mad at Dad, wondering when she would collapse; wondering if I would have to help Dad carry her upstairs.

But instead of telling anyone the truth I make my excuses and escape to the girls toilets in school until it's time for the next class to begin.

One day in school my English teacher Miss Rose asked me if everything was okay. I didn't feel it would be right for me to say anything about the weekend...the party...my Mum. Miss Rose was one of Mum's colleagues - how could I tell her the truth?

So, instead I smiled at her and told her I'd had a great weekend as Mum and Dad had another one of their amazing parties!

As soon as I said it I burst into tears.

Miss Rose was very kind and quietly told me she understood. She went on to explain to me that the reason I had started to cry was because my body was tired of me pretending things were okay when they really weren't.

She was right. I hated the parties. I hated seeing my Dad so worried for Mum. I became really scared when Mum had been drinking – I didn't recognise her anymore. Mum didn't look, act, or even sound the same once she had taken that first drink.

Miss Rose asked me if I'd like to speak to someone about it. I was a bit worried about Mum finding out, but she reassured me that it would be completely confidential. She even told me that I didn't have to tell Mum about the meetings and the person I spoke with would keep everything I said private - just between me and them. I agreed to see someone, and as soon as I did I felt like a huge weight had been lifted off my shoulders.

The next week a lady called Ann-Marie came and met me in the private meeting room at school. She was from a group called Al-Anon & Al-Ateen.

I had never heard of it before. Ann-Marie was young and pretty. I had expected an old man with a bow tie, someone very serious, ancient and with a musty smell about him – she was not what I'd expected at all!

Ann-Marie told me what the organisation was all about.

Al-Anon was run by people who had someone in their family who drank too much. It didn't matter who it was - it could be a Mum, Dad, brother, sister, Grandma, Uncle - whoever it was it would have an effect on the whole family. Ann-Marie was really easy to talk to, and she totally understood my situation with Mum.

Al-Anon had meetings regularly where everyone had the chance to speak about what was going on with the member of their family who drank too much and how it was affecting them – they supported each other. Al-Ateen was the same only it was for young people, like me. I was relieved, excited and amazed that these organisations existed and that I could meet other people who would understand what I was going through! I couldn't believe it – I wasn't alone after all!

Ann-Marie explained that when someone can't control the amount they drink, and when it's affecting their lives to the extent Mum's drinking was affecting us they call the condition alcoholism. I'd heard of alcoholism in Social Education class, but I thought alcoholics were those poor homeless people who just drank cheap, strong cider or vodka straight out the bottle so as to escape from their horrible, difficult lives. Ann-Marie assured me alcoholism was not an illness that had any "class" boundaries – it affects many, many people in the world from the wealthiest to the poorest.

Ann-Marie told me that the local Al-Ateen meeting took place on a Wednesday night and if I wanted to go she would pick me up and bring me back home. I felt excited and nervous all at the same time! I told her I'd love to go and I'd see her then.

When I got home that night I told my Mum and Dad about Ann-Marie, and the meeting on Wednesday night. Ann-Marie had explained that I didn't have to tell Mum and Dad about it, but that decision was entirely up to me.

Mum cried. Dad told me later it was because
she hadn't realised her drinking made me unhappy
and confused. She didn't say anything to me though.

I slept well that night, it was the first time in ages – I hadn't realised just how frightened I was of Mum's drinking until I spoke about it to someone.

Wednesday never seemed to arrive. I didn't really know what to expect, but I was looking forward to it … in a strange sort of way!

Ann-Marie came and picked me up to take me to my first meeting.

She was lovely and seemed to know, without me saying anything, that I was nervous about what would happen there.

She reassured me and told me that I would meet people who knew exactly what I felt like but still I could feel myself starting to get a headache and feel quite tense about the meeting.

When we arrived a young man met me and shook my hand welcoming me to the meeting and hugging Ann-Marie, they seemed to know each other well. There were about 7 people all sitting round chatting and smiling as I walked in. One girl approached me and asked me if I was new to Al-Ateen; I nodded. She asked if I'd like to sit next to her, which I did. Everyone seemed so friendly!

The meeting started with one person speaking and welcoming everyone and then one by one the 7 people introduced themselves and started talking.

Some of them only said a few words about how they were feeling, others spoke about the day they'd had and how the alcoholic in their lives had been recently. No one said anything bad about the person whose drinking affected their lives – there was a real sense of sadness about their drinking, but not anger towards them.

I was so glad about that, because I had been really worried about what to expect at the meeting. I had been scared that I would be expected to hate my Mum and be rude about her in some way, blaming her for me being tired at school and having a sore tummy when I was frightened by her drinking. Instead, I could be sad about her being an alcoholic, speak about how I was feeling and know that these people in the room totally understood my sadness.

Ann-Marie drove me home after the meeting – I felt amazing! My headache and tension had gone and I couldn't believe that alcoholism affected people in the same way. I had been given the opportunity to speak about how I had really been feeling. My emotional and physical pain had lifted as I'd done that.

One thing that they did make clear during the meeting was that it wasn't our job to try to change the drinker in our lives – they were the only ones who could do that.

It was important that we supported each other, so two of the girls gave me their phone numbers and told me to ring them anytime I felt scared or upset by Mum's drinking. The Al-Ateen members explained that we have to be able to get our needs met and keep ourselves safe – I felt cared for and understood, and I was enjoying it!

During the meeting I heard other people speak about their fear when their Mum/Dad/brother came in drunk, or lay sleeping in a drunken state on the floor in the living-room – and I could identify with it all.

I had felt so isolated before Miss Rose had spoken to me in school, but now I felt so supported I was incredibly grateful for being told about this organisation.

When Ann-Marie dropped me off we made arrangements for her to collect me again for the meeting the following week. I had found a way of letting out how I'd been feeling and I wasn't about to give that up – not when it made me feel so good!

Mum and Dad were waiting up for me when I got in. Mum was sitting at the kitchen table – she looked really upset.

I felt my heart sink, but I knew I had to tell her how the meeting went as she wanted to know.

I made the point of making sure she knew I didn't spend the time saying bad things about her. I told her that the meeting meant that I could speak about my worries about her and about my hope that one day she would find a way of stopping – but that I also knew only she could do that.

She gave me a hug and didn't ask me any more about it. Dad hugged me too and told me he was proud of me for going.

Mum and Dad still have parties.

Sometimes I go and stay at a friend's house, and sometimes I just go to bed early.

Every Wednesday I go to the Al-Ateen meetings and talk about how I'm feeling, and how my Mum has been.

I tell my Mum how I feel now, where before I wouldn't have felt able to tell her how sad it made me when she'd been drinking.

I feel much better when I'm at school: I don't get a sore tummy anymore, and if I feel nervous about one of their parties coming up I tell them about it and that always helps me feel better.

I still hope that one day Mum will admit to herself she's got a problem with her drinking and go and get some help from her Doctor or Alcoholics Anonymous.

No-one can make her do that: she has to want to do it for herself.
I love my Mum and Dad – I just don't like their parties.

Help & Support
For Friends & Families of Alcoholics

www.al-anon.alteen.org

www.al-anon.alateen.org.uk

Help & Support For Alcoholics

www.alcoholics-anonymous.org

www.alcoholics-anonymous.org.uk

UK National Helpline:

0845 769 7555

Other Useful Websites

www.reverse-therapy.com

www.kathleenhaden.com

About the Author

Kathleen was born in 1968 in Bowmore on the Scottish west coast Island of Islay.

On the 4th May 2004 Kathleen attended her first Alcoholics Anonymous meeting following years of dealing with the problems that alcohol brought to her family.

She now lives with her three children in Kirriemuir, Angus and runs 3 Reverse Therapy clinics in Dundee, Edinburgh, Shetland and Harley Street, London.

Kathleen hopes that this book helps others find hope with alcohol related difficulties in their lives.